MY BEST FRIEND IS WHITE

Klyde Broox

I dedicate this collection to Joan, Tia, Theo and Tayo,
who have also paid the considerable opportunity cost
it took to arrive at this book. **KB**

Library and Archives Canada Cataloguing in Publication

Broox, Klyde
    My best friend is white / Klyde Broox.

Poems.
ISBN 1-894692-13-6

    I. Title.

PS8603.R668M9 2005   C811'.6   C2005-904252-4

Printed in Canada

Editor: Lillian Allen
Copy Editor: Sandra Alland
Cover Design: Danilo McDowell-McCallum
Inside Layout: Heather Guylar
Cover Illustration: Danito McDowell-McCallum
Author Photo: Ian Gibbons
Copyright © 2005, Klyde Broox

In the poem "Marley Vibe," lyrics have been quoted from the songs of the late Bob
Marley, in particular phrases in common usage in Jamaica.

Canada Council   Conseil des Arts
for the Arts   du Canada

CONTENTS

A DUBPOET DECLARES

The title, *My Best Friend is White*, sends an exhilarating surge of tension in my veins, a strong sense of adventure. When I mentioned it to a black friend, she asked if I had the courage to be a dubpoet carrying such a title. My answer was simple: "Well, I had the guts to write the poem." Another friend (who is white) suggested that I should think of another title if I wanted this book to be embraced by Jamaicans. Once again my answer was simple, with a little chuckle and a bit of self-caricaturization thrown in that time: "Jamaica, no problem mon, the national motto is: 'out of many, one people.'"

So why should I think about changing the title or finding extra courage to carry it? The poems in this book respond comprehensively to that two-pronged question. With the guidance of my editor, Lillian Allen, I have attempted to imprint (dub) onto the page, scribal recordings/re-recordings, duplications, replications, explications, collations, and extrapolations of daily realities in Canada and Jamaica under the Earth's single sky. The actual title poem was written by incident (a common feature of dub). At home, I often invade my kids' televisionspace with comments on colour-coding in the media. One night, my son, who was then ten years old, asked me with the sincere point-blank-matter-of-factness that only children can administer, how I can be so "black conscious" with a "white best friend." The question felt so profoundly insightful that I had to stay up late that night to write the poem, "My Best Friend is White." Dropping that pebble created the strengthening ripple which is now the title of my first real collection of poetry (honourably excepting the fabulously well-received underground gem, the rough and raw sub-industry standard '89 chapbook, "Poemstorm").

The trajectory of this book's title is particularly significant in comparison to some earlier dub-books like: *Dread Beat An' Blood* (Linton Kwesi Johnson); *Echo* (Oku Onuora), *Outcry (*Mutabaraka); *It A Come* (Mikey Smith); *Rhythm An' Hardtimes* (Lillian Allen); *Riddym Ravings* (Jean 'Binta' Breeze); and *Earth Woman* (Cherry Natural). We can see an incremental reconfiguration of metaphor beginning with the title, *Rhythm An' Hardtimes*; another increment evident in the stylistically connotative *Riddym Ravings*. Then, *Earth Woman* paves the way for *My Best Friend is White*. The fact that the three books in question were published by dubwomen can be seen as a result of the essential need for feminist philosophy to transcend boundaries that limit the spread of universal sisterly solidarity. This book is also geared to transcending boundaries.

The story of dub poetry continues to write itself through its poets. *My Best Friend is White* could well be the title of a new chapter of the dubstory: "The Transcultural Phase." This title of an essay by the widely quoted German academic-dubresearcher-dubbedpoet-socasinger, Christian Habekost, suggests his awareness of this reality and underlines the obviousness of dub's intercultural validity. A major aim of the title, *My Best Friend is White,* is to de-otherize the book in the domains of a separated white reality that would relegate dub to a niche minority market. From where I stand, the fact that the publisher is white presents an example of the alliance that Habekost's essay title implies.

The employment of strategic initiatives to further engage white people in the black discourse on race, in a white-dominated world, is not new. Dub poets have always projected visions of a general Tellurian family, perhaps never before from the bridge of bestfriendship, but certainly always aiming to establish a balance of equality for all peoples. One has to be a person first before one can fall into any of the many categories of social differentiation and stratification that divide us among ourselves to frame us as minorities and marginalize our humanity. I therefore refuse to feel like a minority in the company of other persons.

As black Canadians continue to strive for more inclusion in the broader discourses of mainstream white-majority-conditioned society, it is in our best interest to provide pathways for reciprocity. We — both blacks and whites — should strive to divert the parallel lines of cosmetically separated Canadian discourses on race, to construct points of convergence where widening fields of livalogue can neutralize othering and promote solidarity. I write and chant to invoke a sense of social engagement that is not restricted by cultural corridization. My utterances are consciously framed to deterritorialize struggle, and cast everything in the light of the overstanding that we are all just tellurians, inhabitants of a village in space called Earth. Here is a poet whose village is a planet.

Blah-blah, reh-reh, yeah-yeah. After all the artification of statement and the stylization of protest, when the hand holding is over, if push comes to shove, my white best friend and I know that together we can fight for equal rights and justice, side by side, until skin colour is as meaningless as shades of iris. So, where are we now in terms of dub? I would say that, despite the fact that Jamaica continues to be the main engine of dub, the efforts of the Dub Poets Collective locate Canada as the current undisputable hub of the present international dub poetry movement. For me, this arrival at a point of diasporic centrality is an valid, and too long deferred claim on a leadership role in the Black Diaspora.

And where is this growing sense of black Canadian cultural nationalism and Pan-Africanist confidence coming from? I attribute it equally to the resilience of "native" black Canadians and the strengthening of the Caribbean presence in the psyche of contemporary Canada. Canadian dub poetry dramatizes and problematizes the complexities of black "Canadianality"; to an equal extent it also analyzes the global historical responsibilities of Canada and Canadians in a more polarized post-9/11 world. On today's Earth we need, more than ever before, to transform the spectacle of the other into the notion of the also. We all seem to have lost a little bit of ourselves under the misdirection of polarity. Dubbing gives us the option of converting cultural collisions into grooves that punctuate a fascinating dance of mutual self-recovery "under the influence of dub."

And what is dubpoetry really? Dubpoetry is the blending of musical, literary, and oral storytelling devices with vernacular speech rhythms. It is different from other spokenword styles because it is driven by a sense of dreadness that is rooted in Rasta/reggae tradition. Dubpoetry can also be defined by most of the dictionary and colloquial meanings of dub. Ultimately, dubpoetry is both the scripting of orality and the oralizing of scribality. For dubpoets, the stage is a page and the page is a stage. This chiasmic reality holds true in many cases: voice as pen/pen as voice, uttering to write/writing for utterance, agonies of comedies/comedies of agonies, sound of dub/dub of sound, poetic body/body poetic, dub as poetry/poetry as dub. It is perhaps possible to be confused by this duality, however I interpret it as a sense of balance.

"Dubwise" can be read as being mimetic, an editable and updateable mirror. In dubpoetry, use of language is resoundingly intentional. Dubpoets employ constructionist approaches to meaning in language and dub blends well with the Saussurean notion of underlying codes and structures. Dubpoets fuse mimetic/reflective, semiotic, intentional, structuralist and constructionist approaches to language. This fusion seems at once synthetical and synergistic, because it references both theory and practice simultaneously. Dubpoetry also incorporates a great deal of "overstanding," which provides both worm's eye and bird's eye views in a single glance. (NB: "overstanding" — an original Rastafarian concept — is the comprehension of the relativity of epistemologies and the subjectivity of ideologies.) Dub is more than postcolonial; it is countercolonial, moving towards "noncolonlality."

To those who have known me from back in the day, in Jamaica, I say, this is Durm-I updated, very 21st Century: from "The World Is Too White" to "My Best Friend Is White." Many of the poems in this book migrated with me from Jamaica. Most of them are self-evident, but

"Color TV" deserves special mention because its root version origi-nated in Jamaica and it was translocated to directly address the need for "more people like me/ on my color TV," in the North American context. "Misery Rime" was also born in Jamaica. It is particularly spe-cial to me because it was the poem that made me conscious of the fact that I could try to make people laugh instead of cry. Its numerous versions also track my ideological growth to a level of heightened sensitivity to diverse sensibilities.

Apart from racists, "downpressors," and rapacious capitalists, I don't want to make anyone feel uneasy. However, I don't necessarily write what I think people want to hear; I write what I feel needs to be said. If a poem demands to be written, I have to write it. Therefore, "My Best Friend is White," but my God still "talk patois," and I am proposing the "mutiny of the subaltern." Also, since the whole world now lives "in the shadow of America," I am gravely concerned about the immensity and offensiveness of "the American war machine." I think we should always be vigilant about how when and why it is de-ployed, especially since it will have to lead us "if Mars attacks." Finally, about dubpoets in general, I would say, even when it seems that we're making jokes, we're not kidding because; "the world's moving so fast/ the next minute/might be a big bomblast/to ra-ha-ha-ha-sssss …

Seriously,
Klyde (Durm-I) Broox
@ the hub of the dub, DPC office
Toronto, August, 2005.

INTRODUCTION

In an unlooked-for burst of rhythm from Hamilton, a rapid-fire salvo of rhymes announces Klyde Broox, dub poet. A well-loved landmark in the southern Ontario performance scene, Broox believes in the power of word-art to fight oppression and right injustice. Intensely allusive, multi-layered, skillful, and unfailing in its sense of comic timing and rhetorical positioning, this poetry cannot fail to change Canadians' perspective on Canada, its literature, and its historical and political relationship with the African diaspora. Canada is particularly fortunate in Broox; its imagination is being educated in startling and important ways.

Broox's analysis of European-African historical relationships informs poems against American cultural and trade imperialism, against gun violence, against the pretentious "paperpoets" of the official literary imagination, and diverse facets of Canadian racism. This racism, limned with wit and perception, appears in these poems in all of its "maple-syrup-coated" Canadian denial, its production of a peculiar combination of hypervisibility and invisibility for black people, and its ironies when considered against the original historical alienation of slavery ("Sumadi Mus Kno Mi Name"). The poem "Hyphenation" comments on the situation of hundreds of thousands of professionals – health professionals, teachers, engineers – who have migrated to Canada only to have their professional qualifications invalidated, and who are struggling to make ends meet on clerical or manual labour. "There is more than sweat to offer," writes the poet, and he makes good on that declaration in this book.

In "Glimpses and Glances," lyrical, evocative lines create a portrait of the Caribbean immigrant's relationship to Canadian winter that is reminiscent of Dionne Brand's in *Winter Epigrams*. In these similarly rueful, though differently crafted lines, "Shovelling for poems on frostbitten deck / Fragments of the past I recollect / ... / Sunshine creased into memories," a clash of winter with the tropics' eternal summer rubs elbows with the simple, wispy fantasy: "I wish I'd learned to dance on skates." Broox also shares with Brand a sensitivity to images and meanings of the word "skin" in a racist culture: "Stains of unequal meaning / Degraded shades of skin / Paperthin sense of belonging." In "Sumadi Mus Kno Mi Name," what begins as the alienation of a Caribbean immigrant to Canada ends as the alienation of a deracinated African, so that home recedes in a double wave of disorientation and enervated longing.

Like all dub poets, Broox combines concrete details of the local and the everyday — television programming, the Internet, employment conditions, and current events — with sophisticated political analysis. Often this analysis is accomplished with Latinate words whose abstract semantic field is an integral part of the dub: "Expressway to further pollution / Sometimes election is selection / Twisted arms of objection / Distorted common opinion / Lip service to the Iroquois / Grinning teeth of chainsaw"("Red Hill Chainsaw Massacre"). The three-syllable words ending in "-ection" would create feminine rhymes in my English. In Broox's Jamaican, they create a set of rapid beats sweeping the reader-listener through a closely argued analysis. Broox integrates extremes of diction into almost every poem, a feat that places him both within and at the forefront of the Jamaican literary tradition.

Jamaican poets use Jamaican language through all of its Atlantic-wide ranges. What is distinctive about Jamaican language is not only its vowels and rhythms, but also the range of its verbal artists, who, when it suits their poetic purposes, set the most Queenly of English alongside the rootsiest Afro-Jamaican. And because Afro-Jamaican is still largely unstandardized, though often written, dub poets create a rich magic when they integrate the living orality of Afro-Jamaican into an emerging written literature. For some readers, this will mean making a slight though conscious effort to make the strange into the familiar. Knowledge of the words, "fi" ("to" or "for"), "oonu" ("you all" or plural "you"), and "deh" (present progressive) help to bring out the pathos of the reggae poem "Teacha Still Deh Teach," for example. With this gloss, the refrain "Soh Teacha still deh teach / Deh teach, deh teach" becomes clearer for the non-Jamaican reader as a rocking lullaby about the slow-moving circle of education: "So Teacher is still teaching, teaching, teaching." It is worth remembering, too, that in Jamaican, "war" rhymes with "car," "teeth" with "street," "Indian" with "land," "deck" with "recollect," "about" with "mouth." For a reader who has not heard Jamaican, though, these lines still scan, if a little differently. The dub rhythm carries all before it.

Broox is a classic dub poet; much of his sound inspiration draws on Bob Marley and the Last Poets. His performance persona is good-humoured, unassuming, without backup sound or effects. Every piece is carried forward on the sure, infectious beat of his voice. Repetitions are important to that beat, and his poetry exploits repetition brilliantly on a number of levels, from passage to single sound. In "The Revolution Has Changed," Broox weaves a path through infinitesimal changes in rhythm along a line of strict repetition, a feat of sound-in-writing reminiscent of the early Gertrude Stein. Repetitions are often varied with mid-line commas that work like the caesuras of beat-heavy Anglo-Saxon poetry: "My best friend, is white / My best friend is white" ("My Best Friend is White"). In the hard-hitting "Until," three-beat lines structured by alliteration create another striking resemblance to Anglo-Saxon prosody: "Homes of the helpless burning / Mothers of the murdered mourning / … / Weeping widows wailing / … / Misery's minstrels lament."

First cousin to repetition, related through the ritual roots of poetry-as-chant, the namings – the lists of names – in many of these poems create similar sound-and-meaning effects. A list of African place names in "Afroscope," reminiscent of Edward Kamau Brathwaite's *The Arrivants,* evokes another, African universe of culture and language. Like M. NourbeSe Philip's gropings for a forgotten African language, these names allow a temporary conjuring of a lost world: "Congo, Nile, Niger / Oil-rich Sahara / Kilimanjaro, Mount Kenya / Sunlit savannah." Another function of the name-list is genealogy, and "Afroscope" also contains a genealogy that sets the poet and his family into an oral-historical tradition: "Struggles of blackwomen like Joan Brooks / … / The mighty Maroon Queen: Nanny / Garvey, Bob Marley / Muhammad Ali / Malcolm X, Martin Luther / Nefertiti, Winnie, Oprah / W.E., Booker T. / His Imperial Majesty: Haile Selassie."

Perspective also motivates the listing technique, for of all the possible "scopes" the title suggests, only the kaleidoscope constantly arranges the shattered pieces of a world into patterns of beauty. All of the name-lists in this poem rearrange, like a kaleidoscope, the European logic that has created a twisted perspective on Africa: "A place of perennial sunlight / Blindly compared to night / Snow-white heart of darkness." Shifts in perspective also drive poems like "My Best Friend is White," a study in symmetrical dualities: white and black, best friend and white, black and friend, black and white. In the childlike "Freddy's Daddy," an absent, deadbeat (or worse) dad is presented through the eyes of his inquiring son, Freddy. Finally, "There Was Another Indian" is an eerie poem about the "Indian" who understood the implications when he saw Columbus make landfall. He "Told himself goodbye and was about to leap / Out of his own life" but in the end, he simply went home. The poem creates an absence, an alternative, just barely glimpsed during an infinitely receding moment.

Working with and against cultural images and their distortions is one of Broox's strong suits. While some lines create sudden changes in perspective, others directly name the problem: "Despite the Underground Railway / There has always been a colour code." In "Soulscape Online," ubiquitous acronyms are deliberately distorted for a startling effect: "HolyTalk Magic Language / HyperTruth Transmission Process / Flexible-Transfer Protocol."

A dedication to Maya Angelou and poetic dialogues with hip-hop poets, dub poets, and other black artists reveal Broox's embeddedness in a rich, New World African imaginative tradition. His filial literary relationship to Louise Bennett is clear in "Cow an Goat Style," a rhythmically fantastic, rollicking poem in broad Jamaican, which in its chorus gently satirizes Lillian Allen's "Rub A Dub Style Inna Regent Park": "Minibus ride inna cow an goat style / Wickid an wile, keep yuh frettin evri mile." Like Jean 'Binta' Breeze, he has created a heartfelt lament for Mikey Smith, in "Mi Cyaan Believe It Yet." Smith, a contemporary of both Breeze and Broox, was murdered on the street for voicing criticism of a political candidate running for election.

Chattel slavery is an important organizing trope of the New World African imagination; with "Priz'n Islan," Broox adds a distinctive lament that focuses on the existential constriction and hopelessness of enslavement. Unlike the stereotypical male dub poet, there are few furious rants among these poems. One sincere rant is about the visceral experience of poverty hunger ("Dubmuzik on the Street"). Another, "Slam-Poem!" ends in gentle self-mockery: "And whether you like it or not / I'm giving it everything I've got / Because only an idiot or a loser / Would whisper in a slam / Poem." Broox persuades by educating; his didacticism is always sensitive to audience, and laced with humour and gentleness.

In company with Lillian Allen, Chet Singh, Afua Cooper, Michael St. George, d'bi.young, Clifton Joseph, ahdri zhina mandiela, Devon Haughton, Oni the Haitian sensation, Naila Keleta Mae, Anthony Bansfield, Motion, and others of Toronto's Dub Poets Collective, Klyde Broox offers Canadian poetry a new horizon. Readers familiar with his performance favourites, "Mas(k)culinity," "Literary Coup," "Going Dot Com," "Rant Against Otherness," and "Colour TV" will be overjoyed to find this cache of his "Southern noise in the North."

Maria Caridad Casas
May 2005

UNDER THE INFLUENCE OF DUB

FOREIGN ACCENT

My native voice is my trademark
I don't feel strange when I talk
This accent is no accident
Nor spp-eech impediment
It is not recent, but ancient
It's not something that I invent
So skip the value judgment

Represent, ripresent
Don't have to resent
Stat-us, stay-tus, forget the fuss
No need to be facetious
Self-conscious or supercilious

Leisure, leezure
Free time we treasure
Standard procedure
Not a matter for conjecture

Tomayto, tomaato
Potayto, potaato
Dayta, daata; zed or zee
Still the same vocabulary

Con-tro-ver-sy, controv-ersy
Build a bridge across the sea
Level out the hierarchy
No need to be negative
Language is relative
Distribution of syllabic stress
Should not create ethnic distress

The Queen's English is her own
Let her speak it from her throne
I know my English is fine
I am sure it is mine
And it's not borderline

Alien or ali-an, I don't fit that description
I can prove it in any type of examination
I am a born Tellurian
Citizen of planet Earth, my place of birth

RELOADING THE CAN(N)ON

"So much for deconstruction"
"Time now for reconstruction"
"We don't believe in bloody revolution"
"We have moved on, from Fanon to Anon"

Voices of decolonization
Reloading the can(n)on
With homemade ammunition
Weapons of mass liberation
Weapons of mass liberation

Beat of heart prepares the path
Flow of art from South to North
Songs of peace from West to East
Timeless quest to tame the beast
Shades of gray can pave the way

As a matter of fact
You don't have to be black
To go where Shakespeare meets Tupac
And they split a six-pack
Reloading the can(n)on
With homemade ammunition
Weapons of mass liberation
Weapons of mass liberation

Transpolymotions
Dance across oceans
Translocated traditions
Counterconnotations
Infiltrate imagination
Shift the tide worldwide
Wordwars of representation
Voices of decolonization
Reloading the can(n)on
With homemade ammunition
Weapons of mass liberation
Weapons of mass liberation

Tell the keepers of the gate
Freedom won't wait

UNDER THE INFLUENCE OF DUB

Sweet and sour jerked-around blues
Moody migratory vernacular muse
Creole soul, raw, soul Creole
Southern noise in the North
Southernoising the North
Under the influence of dub

Under the influence of dub
Bodyspeakers
Demolish language barriers
Illuminate ivory towers
Accelerating rates of insight
Obscurity obliterated by spotlight
Under the influence of dub
Dub, dub
Dubculture is not shrubculture
Not a scrubculture, no grubculture
Nor paystubculture
Not much of a pubculture
Nor fanclubculture
Dub, dub
Dub is subculture, hubculture
Voice signature, live literature
Altercultural capital
Ancestral oracular revival
Surviving a continual spiral
Under the influence of dub

Digital camera
Upgrade your browser
Gestures popular, unheard murmur
Bodies politic talk louder
Under the influence of dub

Close encounters of an oral kind
Open the windows of a shuttered mind
Powers and forces realigned
Under the influence of dub
Dub, dub,
Dubber dubbing
Dub, dub,
Dub-in, dub-out

AFROSCOPE

Congo, Nile, Niger
Oil-rich Sahara
Kilimanjaro, Mount Kenya
Sunlit savannah
Leopard, lion, tiger
Elephant, panther
Cheetah, hyena
Gazelle, giraffe, zebra
Et cetera, et cetera

Woe wails from the Horn of Africa
Gold and Ivory Coast haunted by greed
Ghosts of colonies linger
So many mouths to feed
Modern Africa in need

Overshadowed contours, tainted grandeur
Impoverished postures, hopeless hunger
Naturally rich, politically bewitched
African enigma, Pandora's panorama

Post-colonial reality: grief and misery
Africa seen as a hard place to live
Primitive, jungle, poverty, struggle
Apartheid, IMF, AIDS, thatch hut
Drought, famine, desert, wanton revolution
Chaos, dismay, disease, desolation
Millions of orphans

This was not always so
Greatness from long ago
Gong gong, abeng
Africa will rise again

Talking drums, drums talking
Pre-slavery heritage
Uncovered knowledge

Traces of kingdoms past
Axum, Timbuktu, Mali, Ghana
Chad, Songhai, Greater Zimbabwe
Gone but not lost

Africa didn't fall, it got pushed
From First to Third World
Mother Earth, she knows
Of Black Pharaohs
Echoes from ancient Africa
Before there was ever
Even the thought of a nigger

Enter the European
Invasion and dispossession
His story called it discovery
Africa, the "dark continent"
Prelude to enslavement

A place of perennial sunlight
Blindly compared to night
Snow-white heart of darkness
Slave trade, colonialism; rape
Treasures stolen, cultures broken
Unknown tongues spoken
Native foreigners

De-rooted descendants
Cast out across far waters

New Africa in turmoil
Civil wars of ascendancy
Bloody sibling rivalry
Nigeria versus Biafra
Ethiopia against Eritrea
Rwanda, Sierra Leone
Murderous seasons of the gun
More woe in the Congo
Continental lamentation
Slaughter in Sudan

Outcries from Liberia
Coup d'état, martial law
Portraits of self-hate, native bigotry
Whitewashed blackmen, hijackers of liberty
Blood-drenched charades in military khaki

Defiant freedom fighters
Survivors of slave traders
Resistant ancestors
Baobab, spear; Shaka Zulu was there

Maroon, Mau Mau
Rasta, Black Panther
Roots, ancestral worship
Rituals without the whip
Navigation of repatriation
Negotiation for reparation

Black Power for sisters in the Diaspora
Tribute to Sojourner Truth
Ode to the unknown higgler
And a line for my father's mother
I salute you, Maya Angelou
Aunt Ell and Dassie Walker too
My mother, Sylvia Braham
Last daughter of Mumaa Graham
Signs between the lines of history books
Struggles of blackwomen like Joan Brooks

Teach the children to remember
Patrice Lumumba
Jomo Kenyatta, Kwame Nkrumah
Biko, Mandela, Nyerere, Tutu
Moloisi, Saro-Wiwa
Miriam Makeba
Queen of Sheba, Cleopatra
Emperor Sundiata Keita
Mansa Musa, Harriet, Rosa
The mighty Maroon Queen: Nanny
Garvey, Bob Marley
Muhammad Ali

Malcolm X, Martin Luther
Nefertiti, Winnie, Oprah
W.E., Booker T.
His Imperial Majesty: Haile Selassie

So many other heroes
And sheroes like those
As time comes and goes
Examples of a noble
Irrepressible people

Revelations in the Afroscope
Time is longer than rope
Ask the Pope

GETTO LINGOZ

Bu-bu-bu …
Bullit ah spit
Scre-scre-screemin tawgit

Ratta-tatta-tatta
Big gun dem ah chatta
Spredout an skatta
Peace get shatta
Di bakkle get hotta
Det in di arenaaaa … aah
Getto son an dawta
Gettin slawta
Getto, getto, getto lingoz
Murdaruss ekoz, ekoz of terroz
Memriz of sarroz
Getto lingoz, getto lingoz

Woe! Woe!
Woeful sarrow
Funaral tumarrow
Lawd, granny used to bawl
Di getto lingoz
Mama stilla bawl di getto lingoz
Pickney dem ah bawl di getto lingoz
Getto, getto, getto lingoz
Murdaruss ekoz, ekoz of terroz
Memriz of sarroz
Getto lingoz, getto lingoz

Nevva waan tings to go so far
Nevva waan Pardy fi hol-up di bar
Nevva waan Frankie go tief dat car
Nevva waan fi see Shorty
Ded body spred out pon di tar
Nevva waaant di crime an tribal war!
Did want to be a movie star
But getto life is like a gangsta show
Is soh man grow, is dat man know

Tweedle-dee, Tweedle-dum
Harda dey come, harda dey fall
Doan kno demself
Till dem back againse di wall
Laawd ...

MISERY RIME

Jack and Jill went up the hill
To seek thrills with a big bag of pills
They are up there still
Taking an overdose of free will
While Humpty Dumpty family bawl
For Humpty Dumpty didn't really fall
A terrorist shot him off the wall
Emergency operator sleep out the call
All the best doctors and all the best nurses
Couldn't help Humpty Dumpty at all
He died right there in the middle of the mall

Simple Simon turned con man
Also known as a politician
Had a great plan to con a nation
But when the shh …
Shredded paper hit the fan
Simple Simon brandish his resignation
Now he's just a former statesman
Reaping pension

Georgie Porgie, pudding and pie
Seems to be a straight guy
No tite jeans, jherri-curls
But he doesn't dream of kissing girls
And when the boys come out to play
Georgie Porgie doesn't run away
He stays to say that he's gay
So most of the other boys run away
And spoil the day
Yeah, Little Miss Muffet sits on her tuffet
Promoting porn on the Internet
Mary, Mary, still contrary
Is having her test-tube baby
For she prefers to be celibate
Since AIDS is so easy to get

Tom Tom the banker's son
Embezzled a billion, gone on the run
Won't slow down until da money done
Big Boy Blue can't find a clue
Little Jack Horner
Selling crack on the corner

Hey diddle diddle
Topcat quit playing the fiddle
Now he's just blowing the whistle
He … he ... hee
Hickory, Dickory, Dock
A mouse ran up the clock
Tried to turn it back
And died of heart attack

One fine day in June
The dish ran away with the spoon
To get married in Cancún
Another interracial couple
Fleeing from family trouble
Trying to escape somehow
Like the big brown cow
She stuffed steroids
Got paranoid
Jump'd over the moon
Got lost, couldn't find any grass
Starved to death, no burial yet

Pretty Little Bo Peep is cloning her sheep
But she still pops pills to get to sleep
For the world's moving so fast
The next minute
Might be a big bomblast
To ra-ha-ha-ha-sssss ...

Suspicious nerve gas leak
If the truth is what you seek
Don't look for it in Newsweek

ODE TO AN OBDURATE PAPERPOET

Poems without voices
Paper-noises
Have you found your voice yet?
Obdurate paperpoet

Who gives a heck
Where you put your trochaic foot
Too bad if you trip
Over your anapesticidal
Iambic, pentametrical
Oxymoronic, prosodic versification
Grandiloquent pontifications
Entangled in metred syllables

Obdurate paperpoet
Parading punctuation
Showcasing shadow scansion
You hunt pipe dream couplets
Striving to spin "award-winning"
Illusions of meaning

Scanned your oceans, found no treasure
Feet without inches lead to displeasure
Circumcised gesture
Body absence
Essence of your silence

I cannot hear you yet
Oh great, obdurate paperpoet
Before you write again
Reconnect soul to brain
Refrain from words vain
Take a quatrain to Dubville
Shed your shoes
Sip some first-hand blues
Seek substance for each utterance
Aspire to make poems dance

Oh great, obdurate paperpoet!
Outspoken enemy of my stylized noise
I really admire you in one sense
You dare to textualize your intense silence

SLAM-POEM!

This damn poem is a slam-poem
Slam-poem, this is a slam-poem
It's a proud poem, a very loud poem
Dashing from my outspoken pen
This damn poem, is a slam-poem
And a slam-poem is a damn poem
But not every damn poem is a slam-poem
Some damn poems
Cannot withstand a slam

This damn poem is a slam-poem
Slam-poem, this is a slam-poem
I'm talking a strong poem
It should have been a long poem
But it fell apart
So it's somewhat short
And whether you like it or not
I'm giving it everything I've got
Because only an idiot or a loser
Would whisper in a slam
Poem

CLASSIC RHETORIC

It is said that Alexander was great
He is dead, so he's Alexander the Late
Homer's name has always been big
Long, long before his Simpsons gig

Homey has no time for
Homer and his odysseys
Official mythologies
Pythagoras's accolades
For Euclid and Archimedes
I have some choice phrases
For those lauded and applauded
Thieves of theories
Oh please, put them in a deepfreeze
With Aristophanes and his comedies
They would really suck at Yuk-Yuk's
Never mind Euripides and Sophocles
They were into tragedies

So much for the ways of ancient Greeks
These are the days of computer geeks
Linux, Windows, or Apple?
A question my kids find simple
Would befuddle Aristotle
Xbox, PlayStation, Nintendo?
Don't ask Socrates or Plato

I can hear Chaucer as a rapper
Do you think that he would lip-synch?
Does the Oscar go to Spielberg or Shakespeare?
Can you imagine?
Browning and Keats, reloaded
Head to head pay-per-view slam
Slanging verses of curses to looped beats
Frantic, not Romantic
Rhymes of post-9/11 paradigms

What was hidden from ancient prudence
Now revealed to recent students
But information is not knowledge
Wisdom's not taught in college
And if I were a literary critic
I'd say that this is classic rhetoric

GOING DOT COM

Dear Sir/Madam
I don't give a damn
If you don't care who I am
Or where I'm from
I don't give a damn
If you think it's a sham
Or some sort of scam
Going dot com, I am going dot com

It may be in vain
I might be going insane
Still going to get my own domain
Hi-tech stocks can jump or drop
Some sales-sites shall shut shop
Many e-businesses will surely flop
But I won't stop going dot com
I am going dot com

Maybe I won't get a hit
Might be wasting bandwidth
But I don't care a bit
If it puts you in a fit
Just click "exit" and get over it

So long I've been unheard, unseen
Edited from your TV screen
Now online, I am free to jam
Via real-audio program
Live and direct on webcam
Oh yes I am
Going dot com, I am going dot com
Gone further than CD ROM
Going beyond DVD into virtual reality
Going through to Star Trek territory
Going to be some future version of me
Even if it's only a hologram
I don't give a damn
I've gone dot com

SOULSCAPE ONLINE

Person to person
Voice-dial-up
Heart to heart
Speed of thought
Connection
Domain Naming System
Override
Headspace verified
Pre-initialized
Self-censored search engine
Activated
Built-in backup system
Embedded
Heartbeat rhythm
Stabilized at infinite vibes per second

Common Gateway Interaction
Arbitrary log-in recognition
Love is the password
Let it be seen as well as heard

Global villagers
Bearing animated gifts
Linking priorities
Across continental rifts
Bypass the proxies
Skip the e-business
Let's just trade some cookies

HolyTalk Magic Language
HyperTruth Transmission Process
Flexible-Transfer Protocol
Registration optional

Integrated opensource servers
Universal Response Locators
Reciprocal Access Memory
Cross-spiritual platform interface
Vital rituals based in cyberspace
Earth-anchored mainframe of references
Unlimited network preferences
Updated dreaming, in real time streaming
Soulscape online, user friendly design

Upload, download
Keep your eyes on the road
Decode with mental filter

Hardware, software
Freeware, shareware
Adware, pornware
Spyware, spamware, malware
Beware
Nightmare

Computers can think
Quicker than a wink
But common sense?
Artificial intelligence still too dense

Garbage in, garbage out
Face to face erases doubt
Antivirus, antibug
Please God, don't pull the plug

HYPHENATION

WAT A HIST'RY

From Nanny to Bustamante
Rite up now to you an mi
Wat a hist'ry, wat a hist'ry
Wat a hist'ry!

From slave ship to scholarship
From darknite to satellite
From quadrille to reggae
From coronation to Independence Day
From white missionary
To Honorebel Congo Natty
From so-soh obeah to computer
No more horse an buggy, now is Air Jamaica
From buckymassa to millionaire higgla
From British poun to fi we own Jamaica dollar
From slavery to democracy
From Nanny to Lady Bustamante
Rite up thru Miss Lou an Ranny
Wat a hist'ry, wat a hist'ry
Wat a hist'ry!

From Maroon to Rasta
Slave Boy to Joshua
Hugh Shearer, Eddie Seaga
From Claude McKay to PJ
From ole Naygon to Don Dadda
Roots, rock, Jah-mecca, Little Africa

Sufferin, injustice
Diss, crimination, downpression
Prejudice, poverty an brutality
Couldn't stop wi, couldn't stop wi
Couldn't stop wi
From Nambo Roy to Edna Manley
Rite up thru Sly an Robbie
Wat a hist'ry, wat a hist'ry
Wat a hist'ry!

From plantation sistim to tourism
From chasin duppy to Olympic glory
From Anancy story to Jimmy Cliff movie
From Shakespeare to Dubpoetry
Wat a hist'ry, wat a hist'ry, wat a hist'ry
Wat a hi-story!

The mighty Nanny
Is Jamaica everlasting granny
Daddy Sam Sharpe
Did prefer
Be in his grave than being a slave
Paul Bogle
Give im life to di struggle
For the freedom of black people
George William Gordon
Im nevva ask no pard'n
Marcus Garvey teach black dignity
Bustamante and Norman Manley
Pull down crown colony
Leave equal rights and liberty
Fi all-a-wi, like how Bob Marley
Leave di reggae stylee
Give im son Ziggy
Fi come win up Grammy
Wat a hist'ry, wat a hist'ry
Wat a hist'ry!

From British Empire to Jamaican Diaspora
From Brer Takuma to Shabba
From sidewalk juggler to World Cup baller
From colonial governor
To blackwoman prime minister
From the rule of Britannia
To di rub-a-dub Republic of Jamaica
Wat a hist'ry, wat a hist'ry, wat a hist'ry
Wat a hi-story!

HYPHENATION

English dominion, French connection
Mighty American, regular mention

Oh Canada! I know you remember
Susannah Moodie, pioneer push
Roughing it in the bush
Too real to be "stush"
But, there is more than sweat to offer
Oh Canada, are you reading me?
Tough times in the city
Minus employment equity
Demoted to the shovel
Scraping gravel in a steel factory

So Canada, who is a real Canadian?
Original, ancestral First Nations Canadians
Compartmentalized as Aboriginal-Canadian
Culture-curtained hyphenated nation
Separate corridors for each other-Canadian
French-Canadian, Italian-Canadian
Afro-Canadian, Greco-Canadian
Indio, Latino, Asian-Canadian
Hispanic or Arabic-Canadian
"Exotic" and "ethnic"-Canadian
Jewish-Canadian, Polish-Canadian
Russian-Canadian
Dis-Canadian and dat-Canadian
Another Canadian, Anglo-Canadian
Never heard of such a one
Hyphenation, Hyphenation
Cannot strengthen a nation

Maple-syrup-coated racism
Stains of unequal meaning
Degraded shades of skin
Paperthin sense of belonging
Now Canada, I wonder who really, is a Canadian?
You know, more than just an also-Canadian

Who is not-so-Canadian, hyphenated-Canadian
Underrated-Canadian
Nonwhite, or otherwhite-Canadian
The Canadian
Who is not-quite-Canadian
Hyphenation, hyphenation
Cannot strengthen the nation

PRIZ'N ISLAN

I
Di Afrikan
Ripp'd from
Mama Afrika bosom

Pak'd like contraban
In a slayveship belly-bottom

Get carry beyon, across ocean
Come get bran
Wid whiplash an hot iron
As a slayve pon a priz'n islan
Dat wuz captur'd from
Di Arawak "Indian"

Slayve plantation, Priz'n Islan
Priz'n plantation, slayve islan
Run ... to evri corna
En-up inna ... saltwaata

Saltwaata
Di saltwaata
Too wide to jump ovah
Too deep to get undah
Di saltwaata
Saltwaata wall roun mi ancestah
Trapp'd upon a priz'n islan
Dat wuz captur'd from
Di Arawak "Indian"

Slayve plantation, Priz'n Islan
Priz'n plantation, slayve islan
Run ... to evri corna
En-up inna ... saltwaata

But di sea couldn drown
Emancipation soun
Bloodhoun couldn run wi down

Before wi reach hi-groun
Like Nannytown

Free at laas
Blackskin, white maas
Garvey words come to pass
More rivahs to cross
Di gun dem a blaas
Peter Tosh get shot to rass!

Upon a priz'n islan
Dat wuz captur'd from
Di Arawak "Indian"
Slayve plantation, Priz'n Islan
Priz'n plantation, slayve islan
Run ... to evri corna
En-up inna ... saltwaata

Freedom come wid new barryah
Tings like plane-fare an visa
To fly away from a priz'n islan
Dat di wickid Ol' Madda Inglan
Obtain from Spain by invasion
To retain unda her duminion
Until riot an rebellion
Turn a priz'n plantation
Into a newbran, seconhan, homelan
Where I, di Afrikan
Stilla sing repatriation song
As I trod along pon a priz'n islan
Dat wuz captur'd from
Di Arawak "Indian"

Slayve plantation, Priz'n Islan
Priz'n plantation, slayve islan
Run ... to evri corna
En-up inna ... saltwaata

THERE WAS ANOTHER INDIAN

I've heard that "there was an Indian"
I'm sure there were more than one
And there was another "Indian"
Who saw Columbus land

On cliff-rim, witnessing, a lone
Inhabitant of the "unknown"
He felt no awe at what he saw
His nightmare coming true
Pale strangers from the sea
Cruel conquerors to be
The twist in his story
He knew and understood
Those gigantic
Wind-blown canoes at anchor
Would bring him no good

Evening cloaked in foreboding
No welcoming
Men in too much clothing
People of unusual hue
Splashing eagerly out of the blue
To stick a stick with a painted cloth
Upon his native sand
To claim and rename his land
And to call him "Indian"

Soon, a solemn figure
Perhaps a witch-doctor
One who seemed too weak
To be a cacique
Mimed praises to a god in the sky

The observer on high was moved to weep
Told himself goodbye and was about to leap
Out of his own life
But, on strength of love for his wife
He hurried home instead

Ended up in bed, got laid
And more history was made
For there was another Indian

COLOURED OPINION?

Face to face they call me black
Call me nigger behind my back
Media stereotype, negative hype
Colour screening, glass ceiling
Invisible fences, ethnic streaming
Sometimes I feel like screaming!

When we talk about race
Let's not only dwell on my case
Popular peaceful demonstration
Beyond reservation
Protest the First Nations shituation
Politically tracked, stumbling-blocked
Culture gap, social trap
Struggles for restoration

Is there racism in Canada?
Racism in Canada?
Go figure

Notions of an Irish nigger
Indians who never came from India
Excuse me please, if you are Chinese
See Quong Wing versus the King
Systemic Orientalism

Once upon a Canadian nation
Even the richest Chinese man
Could not hire a white woman
Such men were widely supposed
To be lecherous and treacherous
But still not as bad as us blacks
It can be proven by statistical facts
Black, always rhymes with crack

Is there racism in Canada?
No, never, this is not America
England, New Zealand
Australia or South Africa

There is no racism in Canada
Only subtle threads of xenophobia
Colour-prescribed law and order

Bleached badge of unfair privilege
You know what I'm talking about
Who gets the benefit of the doubt?

Definitely discrete, but still concrete
Where two or more black people meet
Most white people will still choose
To use the other side of the street

Iconography of prejudice
Academic injustice
Some people can't spark
If others aren't dark

Disproportionate
Wages of skin-colouring
Pre-loaded notions that equate
Whiteness and righteousness
Dictates of religious sindicates
Supposing saints who love to hate
In the name of a father that they create

Is there racism in Canada?
Racism, in Canada?
Many will honestly try to deny
Things they find hard to see
Prevalent invisibility factors
Cultural containment corridors

Go ahead and beat your drum
And if some lawmen come
Don't get troublesome; just act dumb

Hidden issues of race in workplace
Whitewashed promotion, Caucasian norm
Could get laid off if you don't conform

Upward mobility?
Restructure your identity
Try to be as white as you wannabe
But those who live to imitate
Will never be great

Talk about a checkered past
Echoes from the Holocaust
Many refused to help the Jews
Racism among whites
Right-wing anti-Semites
Here is a question I have to ask:
Why do they always hide behind a mask?

I've read the book Arabian Nights
Now let's look about Palestinian rights
Honour the United Nations Convention
Equal, universal consideration
Regardless of age, race, gender
Class, religion or sexual orientation
And before I forget to mention
Africa deserves reparation

Of course, it was worse in America
But history does remember
Slavery days in Canada
Source documents have told
That slaves were sold
Despite the Underground Railroad
There has always been a colour code

Parades of charades
Special "multicultural" occasions
"When last did you go home?"
Hyphenation syndrome

Is there racism in Canada?
Of course not, who said that?
Did they say it under oath?
Quote, unquote
Silent majority support?
Let's put it to the vote
Or ask the Supreme Court

Is there racism in Canada?
Racism, in Canada?
Yes, racism in Canada
Some call it a coloured opinion
But it's a fact, not fiction

MY BEST FRIEND IS WHITE

My best friend is white
And I am black
I am black
But my best friend is white

My best friend, is white
But I am black
And racial realities bite
When my white best friend
Reacts typically white
To my coloured insights
About matters of equal rights
I wonder, is my best friend
More white than best friend?
Less best friend than white?

I don't know, maybe
Maybe, I don't know
If my best friend considers me
More black than friend?
Less friend than black?

No stone unturned for honesty's sake
More lessons learned with each mistake
Good friendships may bend
But will not break
I know my friend is not a fake

My best friend, is white
My best friend is white
And I am black
So what?
I am not any less black
Because of that

I am black
And my best friend is white
But that's all right

In my best friend's face
I see what I know to be
Features of one human race
On which I rest my case

AMERICAN WAR MACHINE

Desert brown, jungle green
Navy blue, mountain scene
Air strikes too swift for radar screen
It's the American War Machine
Big, bad and mean
American ... War Machine
Starring the US Marine

Infantry, armoured cavalry
Paratroopers, helicopters, jetfighters
Stealth bombers, airborne-tankers
Rockets, missiles and other projectiles
Aircraft carriers, destroyers
Nuclear submarines
Sneaking beneath sonar screen
The American ... War Machine
American ... War Machine
The American War Machine

Apache, Blackhawk, Cobra
Better not aggravate America

Day and night bombing
High precision targeting
Global positioning satellites
AWAC, unmanned drones
Sooner or later, cyborgs and clones
Chemical-suited universal soldier
Night-vision goggles, body-armour
Made in America, made to conquer

Red, white and blue
Stars and stripes draped over you
Screw the world view
Ain't no stopping those
Awesome American fleets
Of floating battle stations
Hi-tech options

Weapons that can flatten nations
Big, bad and mean
American … War Machine
The American … War Machine

Beat of super-powered war drums
Now here comes another cluster of bombs
Compliments of Uncle Sam
Who is really a humanitarian
Has never knowingly killed a civilian
As we should all take into consideration
Target-sensors work by the numbers
And a number is a number is a number
Whether enemy soldier
Or civilian mother cooking dinner

Strange things happen in the fog of war
But freedom for sale is worth dying for
Despite decimation and devastation
You can bet your life on
Food, water, medical attention
Fabulous fruits of liberation
Loot as much as you can
Learn to shoot like an American

American
The American
War Machine
Terrible, formidable
American ... War Machine
The American War Machine
Ought to have been
Invincible

LIFE IN A NUTSHELL

Life in a nutshell
Not enough heaven
Too much hell
Tomorrow, maybe
Not enough earth, as well

PROGRESS IS A TRAITOR

Progress, oh yes, Progress
Progress is a traitor
A thief and a liar

Mighty machine, virtual being
Push-button realities
Gospels of corporate entities
Counterfeit consciousness
Elevated
Absurdities inverting possibilities
Life stretched beyond meaning

Concrete forests, toxic breeze
Asphalted seas
Cities starving for trees
Dehumanization called civilization
People evolving into integers
Progress, Progress
Oh yes, Progress
Progress is no more babies
Citizen-clones, robodrones
Swarms of android armies
Progress is bomblasted hills
Ocean-staining oil spills
Dome-sealed biozones
Artificial lilies and daffodils
Plastic roses in siliconed valleys
Progress is meals of pills
Synthetic viruses
Smogstain, poison rain
Strained foodchain
Some species won't remain

Progress, oh yes, Progress!
Progress is a traitor
Thief, liar and murdererrr !

RED HILL CHAINSAW MASSACRE

Red Hill chainsaw massacre
                 Red Hill chainsaw massacre
     Arrest demonstrators
Sue protesters
     Police protection for bulldozers
Red Hill chainsaw massacre
                 Red Hill chainsaw massacre

     Strong arms of white man's law
         Lip service to the Iroquois
Can you hear the chainsaw?
            Cut-down forty-four thousand trees
Pass me a gas mask please!
                 Red Hill chainsaw massacre
Red Hill chainsaw massacre

     Scarred escarpment face
Beauty laid waste
     Desecrated tribal sites
Denial of Aboriginal rights
        No more peace in the valley
Indian Removal Policy
     Pave the way for catastrophe
Media bought and paid for
          Democracy, a spectator
Red Hill chainsaw massacre
                 Red Hill chainsaw massacre

Expressway to further pollution
Sometimes election is selection
           Twisted arms of objection
Distorted common opinion
          Lip service to the Iroquois
Grinning teeth of chainsaw
                 Red Hill chainsaw massacre
Red Hill chainsaw massacre

Swapping oxygen for monoxide
Surely seems like suicide
Ecological deficit
Tomorrow does not deserve it

IN THE SHADOW OF AMERICA

Terror for terror is human error
Compassion is a better option

Shuttered windows of opportunity
Ethnocentric homeland security
Failures of foolhardy foreign policy
Gunboat diplomacy, tracks of wrath
Corpse-carpeted warpath
Food, an afterthought
Tentative thanksgiving, no Turkey

Gathering of warwolves
Gulf War sequel, blood-for-oil cartel
Coalition of the ready and willing
Ready and willing to make a killing
Killing for the sake of future drilling

Hasty invasion, dubious grounds
Incoming depleted uranium rounds
Arc of Tomahawk
Downpour of bunker busters
Smart bombs acting dumb
Unholy war
More terror to come
Nowhere to hide, woe for
Children of the other side

Warring armies wave flags
Starving infants swaddled in rags
Shallow graves, body bags
Grief stalks both sides of the fence
Partisan condolence

Eagles landing, plans for re-branding
Wardancing lords of vengeance
Detour to deliverance
Will Uncle Sam go the distance?
Sermons on democracy

Land of new liberty, are you kidding me?
There was also a plan to reconstruct Afghanistan
Gulf War 2, blinkered view
Hegemonic imagery, televisored reality
Scribes of delusion bedded by the Pentagon
History for hire in the shadow of America

Rhetoric aside
War is glorified homicide
And with America allied
You can get killed by your own side
I couldn't blame Canada
For a lack of desire to face further friendly fire

Democracy entails increased cell phone sales
Purse strings attached to the big picture
Taco bells ringing in the future
Post-war Iraq ruled by Big Mac
Incorporated fantasies of big business
Unfounded rumours of cheaper gas

Bloodstained cash
Lightning flash, thunder crash
Two worlds clash
Capitalism versus Islam
We know where Bin Laden came from
We know what happened to Saddam
Don't know what happened to his bomb

No pro-America resolutions
Angry aspersions
"Down United Nations!"
America no longer needs you
Until the bloodbath bills are due

Ashes to ashes, dust to dust
Iraq in chaos
Spin doctors assure us
That great good can come
From freedom in a vacuum
Yeah right, and I was born last night

From what I've gathered so far
It takes more strength to keep the peace
Than what it takes to make a war

IF MARS ATTACKS

Let's imagine at random
If some lethal aliens should come
In this millennium
If Mars attacks, if Mars attacks

If Mars attacks
You know what that means
Invasion by extraterrestrial beings
War machines we've never seen
If Mars attacks, if Mars attacks
We could all get zapped in our tracks
If Mars attacks, if Mars attacks

Watched Star Trek, seen Star Wars
Heard we've sent probes to Mars
Sometimes I'm tense, I can't relax
When I wonder, what if Mars attacks?
If Mars attacks, if Mars attacks

If Mars attacks
That would affect certain facts
With regard to whites and blacks
Rich, poor and whoever
Young or old of any gender
Masculine, feminine or another
Social sector, religious or secular
Wouldn't really matter
Straight, gay or neither
Would have to either run and hide
Or defend Earth together, side by side
If Mars attacks, if Mars attacks

If Mars attacks
Mighty men might melt like wax
If Mars attacks, if Mars attacks
That war would be quite unorthodox
Battles to fight outside the box
If Mars attacks

THE VIEW BENEATH A HARD HAT

JARGON

Dear diary, no new story to be told
Just the same old theory of relativity
One person's fiscal deficit
Is another person's margin of profit

Conservatism, Liberalism
Materialism, Sexism, Racism
Capitalism, Communism, Fascism
Determinism, Fatalism
Random victims of Terrorism

Post-colonialism, out there on a limb
Neo-colonialism looking grim
Searching for a pseudonym

Between organism and mechanism
Ism and schism cause antagonism
Forget ism and step to riddim

Merging conglomerates
Rampaging paper-pirates
Transglobal
Waltz of domination by seduction
Freedom drowning in silicon snake oil
High profile crocodile smile

Information über-highway
Easy to go astray
Digital agenda, Left, Right and Centre
Spam of get-rich-quick scam
Adam Smith must be proud of it

Empowerment, disempowerment
Puppet government
Who knows where the power went?

Time to re-school society
And downsize every army

Isolation, alienation
Technophobia, technophilia
Take no prisoners

Heretics versus fanatics
Diagnostics of pundits and critics
Binary politics
Dialectics of conflicts
So much static can cause panic
Just play I some dubmuzik

Frontiers of the mind
Resistance redesigned
Fighting struggles from databases
Subversive interfaces
Standing tall behind a firewall
Hardware handshaking
Let your fingers do the marching
Attack by e-mail
Mask the modem trail
Hit and run Internet forum
Revolution via public access television

Multimedia guerrillas
Insurgent ideas
Snipers with cameras
Desktop soldiers
Interactive intellectuals
Website generals

Multiracial, intercontinental
Hypertextured countercultures
War of brains, ground the war planes
Fax campaigns leave no bloodstains

Beyond the Great Transformation
Greater expectations
Digitization, automation
Tools of repression and subordination?
Or potential weapons of liberation?

Having waded through all that jargon
We are assured of two main options
Exploitation or emancipation
It's not a matter of opinion
It's our decision

THE REVOLUTION HAS CHANGED

With due respect to Che Guevara
I have a very revolutionary idea
The revolution has changed
Revolution has changed
The revolution, has changed

During the Age of Information
We, the people, have seen
The evolution of revolution
R/evolution, the revolution
Has changed

Revolution has changed
The revolution, has changed
It now involves the machine
Revolution, the revolution
Is no longer red, but green
And the rising rate of inflation
Raises the zillion dollar question
Can you sponsor the revolution?
The revolution?
The revolution has changed
Because change keeps changing
Changing revolution, the revolution
The revolution has changed revolution
R/evolution, the revolution, has changed

Individual revolution
Internal confrontation
Saint against demon
Fighting for self-control
On the battlefield of the soul
My revolution has changed
Because r/evolution *is* change
Change, *change* is the revolution
The revolution?
The revolution is now digitized
Revolution has been revised

Gil Scott-Heron, be advised
The revolution has changed
R/evolution has changed
The revolution has changed
Because … it is being televised

COLOUR TV

I want to see more people like me
On my colour TV
Colour TV, my colour TV
Is not working right
It's showing too much white

I want to see more people like me
On my colour TV, on my colour TV
On my, colour TV I see
Smokescreens, camera tricks
Capitalist symbolism, rat race politics
Sales-slanted special effects
Skewed news, half-baked views
Sophistry, semantics
Slick rhetoric, trick words
Such as "statistics," "demographics"
"Socio-economic logistics"
Spare me the gimmicks

I want to see more people like me
On my colour TV
Colour TV, my colour TV
Is monochromatic
It's too Eurocentric, it must be sick
It seems to me that my colour TV
Is colour prejudiced, it needs to be fixed

I want to see more people like me
On my colour TV, on my colour TV
On my, colour TV I want to see
Twelve months of Blackistry
Bible Days in Afro-reality
On my colour TV, on my colour TV
I want to see Black Enlightenment TV
Better known as B.E.T.
Telling visions of more people like me
On my colour TV, on my colour TV

Colour TV, my colour TV
Has a big   colour problem, so I
Switched it off one night, to write
This protest poem   in black and white

TEACHA STILL DEH TEACH

It ruff inna di chalkduss
But edication is a mus
Soh Teacha still deh teach
Deh teach, deh teach

Teacha still deh teach
Ev'n if di marks dem get
Mek Teacha have to fret
Teacha don't give up yet
For dat is not di firse set
An Teacha still deh teach
Deh teach, deh teach

Students good, students bad
Sumtime dem out fi mek Miss mad
Soh she seh wen dem gaan
She's goin to be glad
But when dem leave, she feel so sad
An only God kno Teacha grief
If anyone of dem go tun tief
For is not dat Teacha teach
An Teacha still deh teach
Deh teach, deh teach

Teacha still deh teach
Teach, teach, teachin ev'n where
Every day is a nitemare
Poor likkle bwoy wid lice in im hair
Pretty likkle girl wid her blouse-bak tear
Skoolshoes dat dun but stilla wear
Plenty pickney lunch money
Haffi use as bus fare
An Teacha really care
But Miss an Sir noh got it fi spare
Mos school need more dess an chair
An some class have to keep in di op'n-air
But Teacha till deh dub it rite in dere
Year after year, nex batch gaan clear

For Teacha still deh teach
Deh teach, deh teach
Teacha still deh teach

Parson deh preach
Salvayshan outa reach
Politician deh beseech
Human rites still deh get breach
Teacha still deh teach
An students deh reach
Some deh reach come teach
An Teacha still deh teach
Deh teach, deh teach

HIPHOPDUB
(A 13-piece hiphop epic)

1 MOTIONS

One-eyed history
Tried to deny our artistry
Lied to label our people as lazy
Belittle our troubles, stifle our struggles
Pin unflattering stereotypes on us
Outcast to typecast
As vicious and dangerous
Or cool clowns in their media circus

Showers of bullets
Versioned disturbances
Punctured resonances
Scattered volleys of utterances
Defiant voices of the Last Poets

Ode to di grandfather
Afrika Bambaataa
Visions of a new Zulu Nation
Rastaman Vibration

Vibes of Natty Dread
Fat Boys, Shinehead
Be quick, or be dead

Fire in di belly
Want to be di nex Nelly
Youtman, be cool
Let Jah rule

Brothers think twice
Most times you have to
Bleed the price
For living in a Gangsta's Paradise

LA ... NY
Let sleeping dogs lie
The faster you live
Is the quicker you die
Pimps and players
Say your prayers

Motions make the movement
Sensations for a moment
Product placement
Pop statement
Arrested Development

So many questions of liberty
Black Like Me
Imprisoned in the land of the free
Profiled as Public Enemy
Said to be a crude nigger with attitude
Branded as bad-ass dude

2 GLITZ

Short run, long run
Blood Run DMC Hammer
Better listen to Mama
Don't run too fast, you might get lost
Beware the glare of glitz and glamour

Bus da rimes
For dollars not dimes
Beat your drums
For perks and plums
Not lemons and limes

At centre stage the blackbird sings
No more puppets on strings
In dese times
"We run tings, tings don't run we"
If you don't believe me, ask P. Diddy
Dollars turn di key, Bad Boy celebrity
Wings of heavy money
Carry levity in di hierarchy

Ice-T, Ice Cube, and a little Brandy
Stretching the vocabulary like Jay Z[ee]
Kriss Kross from Jazzy Jeff to KRS-ONE
And all the unnamed who deserve mention

No more lamentation by the rivers of Babylon
Instead of a rebellion it's a jam session
Sway, like Beyoncé, but don't go astray
Fads and fashions will fade away
But hiphopdub is going to stay

Earlier on the way, there was Dr. Dre
And I dare say, LKJ
Any rime can pay, if it get di airplay
Mi granny us'd to say
"Jus work an pray
Everidog hav dem day"

3 RIDDIM

Ride di riddim an chant along
Sounds of the very strong
Jamaican connection
Yeh mon, Yellowman
Shabba, Sister Nancy
Shaggy, Beenie
Bounty Killer and Sean Paul
After all, hiphop born in a dance hall
Enjoy the gold rush, but remember Peter Tosh

From nude slave beach
To rude stagespeech
Bitter attitudes, angry moods
Deconstructed platitudes

Skip between the black and white
Hop, jump and
Seize the day along with the night

So somehow Eminem
Battled his way into this poem
And now it's too late to stop
The hiphop teeny-bop
Invasion of lily-white suburban lives
Befuddled intellectuals, mesmerized

Bow Wow, wow!
Time to drink milk now
Never mind the mad cow

4 FLAK

ABC, DMX
From auction block
To stock market index
Wanted ... dead or alive
For much more than a
Buck 65

Money in the bank and the pocket
The music business is a corporate racket
Now brotherman is in a different bracket
Got to perform in a flak jacket

Gangster slang, gangbang
Drive-by verse
Arrival in a hearse
Biggie, Tupac!
Black on black gun attack
High-profile tears can't bring them back

One of the things that really bother me
Is how my brothers are so trigger-happy
Daily deaths in our family
Can you hear the guns, hermano?
A loud Latino echo

5 BODYSLAM

Belligerent black, streetbeats
Battering barriers to bits
Driving bigots out of their wits
Bombarding them with hits
Tunes from The Dark Side of the Moon
Curtains of obscurity ripped to shreds
Slavemasters' children bowing their heads
Power of thong, punani-song
Sweetie patootie, beauty of booty
Making money is the first duty
And there is a white girl in the ring
Dancing in a G-string
For she too loves the bling-bling
And she's looking fit
Getting jiggy with it like Will Smith

Bump and grind
From the land of the big behind
Dollar signs on logo-branded minds

Hot claws of sun rake naked backs
Endurance to the max
From railroad to rhythm tracks

Even the def has to jam
To the bodyslam of the battering ram
We all know where these beats came from

Boomerangs of African traditions
There was a time when
Whitemen tried to ban our songs
The abuse of rights is the root of wrongs

6 DEATH ROW

Echoes from Death Row
Where some killer-lyrics flow
Between Sing Sing and diamond ring
"Get rich or die trying!"

7 STORYLINE

Play, fast-forward, rewind
Soulsister, free-up your mind
Like Erykah Badu and Lauryn Hill
Blackwoman, flex your skill
Dance your way off di treadmill
Getto-girl, get up and go
Create your own flow
Glow like J-Lo, climb rainbow

Storylines for all shades of women
Sign your voice with your pen
Like Afua Cooper and Lillian Allen
Keep a Revolutionary Tea Party
Perpetuate sisterstory like Cherry Natural
Inspire Earth Woman revival
Liberate your tongue like d'bi.young
Destiny's chosen child
Streams of consciousness reconciled

8 FREEDOM-MUSIC

ReFugees no more
Unlike those who came before
Shackled and dragged ashore
So don't forget to keep score
On your … big world tour

Horrible
Middle Passage in slaveships
Savage
Language of whips
Speech bondage, shackled lips
Freedom-music in our fingertips

Flash of cleavage
Sway of hips
Right kind of phat
Like Missy Elliot
Too smooth for

Calluses and blisters of slave labours
Ex-blues brothers and sisters
Traveling first class on luxury liners
Along with that, the custom-built yacht

Now, as far as I can tell
Snoop Dogg will never win a Nobel
But he's living pretty darn well
While poets like me struggle like hell
Don't hear any agents ringing my bell

And it's common knowledge
Sometimes "the message"
Is like heavy luggage
But if you've got a grouse
Upstage Mickey Mouse
Make some noise in the house!

9 HOTSTEPPA

Hotsteppa, Salt-n-Pepa
Age ain't nothin but a number
Vaya con Dios, Aaliyah
Glittering eye of shifting camera
White spotlights gaze on Ashanti and Maya
Militant voice-over, Usher in a new era

Young women of colour
Don't bleach and make over
Reach out to take over
Like Queen Latifah, hiphop diva

10 CARGO (1)

Cotton, sugar cane, sun and rain
Flight from pain, midnight train
Buried bodies of memories remain
Slip thru the mesh, Doug E. Fresh
Show me the cash, Grandmaster Flash

Deeper than a shallow glance
I see the Zulu warrior's stance
When rappers dance

11 CARGO (2)

Spirit of a tribal chief
Student of street belief
Captured Negro, American cargo
Shipped to the Caribbean also
Single-parented child of the ghetto
Mother doesn't always know best
So often too young to take the test

12 CASHING IN (1)

Hip-hop hurray for Homey
Hiphoppin thru his life story
Getto biography, Master P
Homey's got to be on MTV!

13 CASHING IN (2)

Six months to peak of fame
Almost everyone knows his name
From 50 Cents to multi-millionaire
Movie deals and custom-wear
Money machine in high gear
Wall Street, GQ, Vanity Fair
Dare to dream despite the nightmare
Get out there and claim your share

Indeed and in truth
If you really want to reap some fruit
It seems best to take the hiphop route
And when it's your turn
To cash in your mout'
Learn how to sell without selling-out

FREDDIE'S DADDY

Now here's a real mystery
Who is Freddie's daddy?
Freddie's daddy?
Freddie's daddy is nobody
And nobody is Freddie's daddy

Every day Freddie
Makes the same inquiry
"Mommy, Mommy, please tell me
Who is my daddy?"
Poor mommy, she can only
Stare at him sorrowfully
Hang her head in misery
Eyes soaked in melancholy
She mutters sadly to Freddie
"Nobody, Freddie, nobody"
Nobody is Freddie's daddy
Freddie's daddy is nobody

Cousin Harry has his daddy
Best friend Larry, he has a daddy
But nobody is Freddie's daddy
Freddie's daddy is nobody

But Teacher says that
"Everybody must have a daddy!"
So every time that Freddie
Goes to visit his granny
He makes the same inquiry
"Granny, Granny, please tell me
Who is my daddy?"
Poor Granny, she can only
Stare at Freddie in misery
Hang her head sorrowfully
Eyes soaked in melancholy
She mumbles sadly to Freddie
"Nobody, Freddie, nobody"

Nobody, mr. nobody
No picture to see
No kind of memory
Only a fading fantasy for Freddie
For Freddie's daddy is nobody
And nobody is Freddie's daddy

WHERE FAMILY GONE

Huge house alone makes no home
Junior faces life on his own
Television was his babysitter
Favourite family member, a computer

Big Brother Wayne
Engaged to Mary Jane
Flirts with cocaine

Sweet sister Charmaine
From limo to jetplane
Stuck in fast lane
Gone with the wind again

Mother hardly there
So busy upscaling career
Living at the pace of a
Recurring rush hour
Hurry, hurry, hurrying
From one appointment to another
Racing herself into therapy

Father locked into latest affair
Has no time to spare
Too busy trying to reach Bel Air
Inbox, outbox, e-mail, fax
Bonds and stocks, Scotch on the rocks

Eventually, of course
Junior, foreseeing a divorce
Writes a bitter question of a letter
Separate copies for
Mother
And father

Hers, on her dresser
His, in the refrigerator

Maybe Junior needs a lawyer
To file for an answer
Where is his family gone?
Family gone, family gone
                    Gone   gone
                                        Gone

GOD IS A DEMOCRAT

The Devil might be a diplomat
But God is a democrat
God is a democrat
I am prepared to vote on that
God is a democrat

Whether he or she
That's another story
But believe you me
God is not a theocrat
Technocrat, plutocrat
Nor aristocrat
God represents the proletariat
I am prepared to vote on that
God is a democrat
God is a democrat

The rule of the rod
Is not the will of God
God is not a dictator
Tyrant, oppressor
Totalitarian, bigot
Not a despot, nor autocrat
Definitely not a bureaucrat
God is a democrat
I am prepared to vote on that
God is a democrat
God is a democrat

If God is a Democrat
Does that make Satan a Republican?
I say yes to that question
And if you want we can
Vote on it in the next election

THE VIEW BENEATH A HARD HAT

It's either too cold or too hot
Stuck in a single spot
Wearing safety glasses, earplugs
Face mask, backstrap, gloves
Tight steel-toe boots
Beneath a hard hat

Punch your time card
Work fast, work hard
Work, work, work
All the way to the graveyard
Life is often like that
Beneath a hard hat

No song in your heart
Not much food for thought
And the breaks are too short
Beneath a hard hat
Where the view is a bit flat

Carry the cross for your boss
Working class
Flesh and blood of industry
Human source of energy
Underpaid proletarian
Only a layoff away from poverty
Just a day-off away from slavery
Yearning to win the next lottery jackpot
Sweating a lot beneath a hard hat
Trying not to think like a bonehead
Although your brain often feels so dead
You'd trade it in for more muscles instead
You use those a lot beneath a hard hat

As the line turns, while the belt hums
OUT truck goes, IN truck comes
No time to twiddle those thumbs
You are just another

Unit of cheap labour
Another pair of hands for hire
Someone the supervisor can fire
Load of a blue collar
Heavy upon your shoulder

Nursing your back
You pace the clock on another
Twelve-hour night shift
Stuck in a single spot
Sweating a lot beneath a hard hat
Hurrying, just to keep your ground
Work, work, working
Toward the next buzzer-sound

GUNSONG

Boom-bang
Dubble-barril gunsong

Easy squeeze, make no riot
This calibre chat is not blank shot
Shot
Shot a lick, shot a lick
Shot a lick like in a war comic

Automatic pistol, remote control
Gunsongs corrupt youtman soul
Make way for di bandalero
Singerman having fun
Slinging songs of the gun

Steel-taloned Desert Eagle
Telescopic rifle
Blood-letting, M16 chorus
Rapid fire, tributes to murder
Shootout showdown
From Brooklyn to Shanty Town
Shot a lick, shot a lick
Shot a lick like in a war comic

Shoot, shoot, shoot and salute
The Great Ooga-Ooga, he loves his Luger
Enter the Lone Ranger with a Ruger
Deadly chatter of the UZI
Voice of a Glock, punch your clock
Heckler & Koch, got a funeral to catch
Three Fifty-Seven Magnum
Death by the gun is often random
Chant of an AK-47
Ain't no Stairway to Heaven

Bob Marley shot the sheriff
Said it was a case of self-defence
Gun violence, a capital offence
Sudden-death sentence
Shot a lick, shot a lick
Shot a lick like in a war comic

Winchester Cathedral
Lethal recital, snipers' central
Full metal teeth of SLR
Pierce your Kevlar even from afar

Here comes a murderer selector
Mr. Quickdraw McGraw, musical outlaw
Show me your Remington
Sounsistim-man

Brandish a gun
-song
Gunsong, gunsong
Gunsongs inspire, young guns for hire
Who labour to retire under heavy gunfire

Gunfire, gunfire
Gunfires ablaze
Targeted nights and days
From getto to getto
Brixton, Kingston, Bronx, Toronto
Woe!
Shot a lick, shot a lick
Shot a lick like in a war comic

Boom-bang
Number-one gunsong
Anthem of a gang
Smith & Wesson riddim section

Dancehall under heat so hot
Johnny Reggae got to get flat
To slip gunshot
Shot

Shot a lick, shot a lick
Shot a lick like in a war comic
Man, woman and child panic
Gunculture problematic
I don't dance to gunmusic

MAS(K)CULINITY

Father, Son and Holy Ghost
Spill some blood and drink a toast
You've got your god to back your boast
An omnipotent man is the lord of host
That's what men have preached the most

Mas(k)culinity, Mas(k)culinity
Don't pin it to the Trinity
Mas(k)culinity, Mas(k)culinity
It has no affinity to divinity
Mas(k)culinity, Mas(k)culinity

Mirrors of mythology
Guy-deology, lie-deology
Sexistology, pseudo-manhood
That's no good

Hollywood male, oh so pale!

Such a tall tale, he's up for sale

Blackmale, whitemale, greymale
All hail from womb of female

Men of steel cannot feel
Mission: Impossible ideal
Totally on reel
Man-ipulations of male ego
Reflection and echo

Music, sex and jewelry
Violence, fast cars and big money
Cameras, drugs and celebrities
Scripted misogynies encrypted in movies
Man-u-fractured personalities
Mirrors of mythology
Mucho machismo por el muchacho
John Wayne, James Bond, Rambo

Shaft, Superfly and Dirty Harry
Guys who never marry
Men without a family
Guts and glory, cock and bull story

Mas(k)culinity, Mas(k)culinity
Don't pin it to the Trinity
Mas(k)culinity, Mas(k)culinity
It has no affinity to divinity
Mas(k)culinity, Mas(k)culinity

Superman, Batman
Spiderman and so on
I have no faith in those
Make-believe superheroes

Johnny Ordinary
Means much more to me
Plain, simple, solid, stable
Unheralded role model
Stifling self to stick to task
Facing life behind a mask
Masks for men, many men in masks
Cheers to the man
Who escaped from a flask

He-man, she-man, not me, man
Just want to be free, man
I won't cast any aspersion
On a next man's orientation

Forget the long argument
But let's not get violent
Let's get anger management

He who needs wide-screen TV
And SUV to feel manly
Will most likely also need therapy
Where is manity, beneath the vanity?
Humanity, few-manity, whose manity?
Time for a new manity

(   )

DEMOKRACY

I know about democracy
About being free, really, really free
Free to an empty belly
Free in your barenaked body
Free to live under a tree
Free, free, freezing or
Freaking out in a demokracy

Democracy, it's a demokracy
Young people free to be hard-core
Free to be their own drugstore
Old people free to sleep outdoor
Baby is free to sleep on the floor
Freedom galore, freedom for sure
If you are not too poor
Or stuck behind a prison door
Free to be, but not to be free
In a democracy, demokracy

Everybody is supposed to be free
Free to diss, dat or di Devil knows wat
But power an money, not free like dat
Few have a lot, most have not
All who cannot abide by dat
Feel free to be a robbin hood, runnin red hot
Free to get SWAT wid a lot of free gunshot
But you won't get a free gravespot
Freedom don't work like dat
It's a demokracy, in a democracy

Wanty-wanty, still needy
Getty-getty, still greedy
Rich people free to make more money
Poor people free to make another baby
What an irony: in a demokracy
Government free to tax everybody
For freedom is not free
It comes with a rising fee

No money, no liberty!
In a democracy, it's a demokracy
Demokracy over democracy
What a hypocrisy, what an irony
What a mockery

UNTIL

Within tumbling waterfalls
Where beauty calls
Grey colours bloom as flowers
Bloodstained scrawls on prison walls
I keep hearing cacophony
Marching soldiers
When the sky sends showers
Rival artillery, explosive tragedy
Bloodwet wind by tumult seasoned
Enemies trade hostilities
Terror's staccato tempo
Echoes from wartorn territories
Fireworks of missiles and rockets
Horror smears the sunset
Danger lurks stark in moonlight
Death at large subdues night
Might masquerades as right
Bomb-laying ironbirds
Blockaded sky
Children crying as they die
Homes of the helpless burning
Mothers of the murdered mourning
More death to greet the morning
Weeping widows wailing
Keening painstroked melody
Misery's minstrels lament
Concurrent bombardment
Barbaric music of conflict
No peace until
Until, until
Until hate embraces goodwill
Or is killed

LITERARY COUP

DUBMUZIK ON THE STREET

Muzik, dubmuzik on the street
Street riddims loud and sweet
Dubmuzik on the street

Magical beat, tonic in the heat
Out on street, raw breeze chafing teeth
Looking for a chance to eat
Eyes don't see it
But feet still have to dance
To the rubadub beat
Loud and sweet, dubmuzik on the street

Daylight well bright, don't want to see it
Forced to greet another sorry sunrise
Belly full with only overnight dubwize

Raw, raggamuffin Reggae
Full blast for breakfast
Two-chord rubadub punch
For lunch, and dinner is the meagre
Leftover lyrics of one more poor
Singing sufferer...er...er
Another dry-bread-night
Drawing nearer…er...er
Angry hunger bubbles in the gut
But
Sounsistims pumping
Basslines jumping
Drumbeats thumping
Hard, dubmuzik on the street
Street riddims loud and sweet
Put me in a trance
Make me jump and prance
Sing and dance
Freelancing to the tune of one more
Insecure, foodhunting evening
Singing and dubbing
Dubbing to the singing

Sing, singer singing
Singing, for a little offering
Lord, I know it's a foolish thing!
To keep wishing that I could really eat
The soursweet dubmuzik on the street

MY GOD TALK PATOIS

My God talk patois
My God talk patois
That is why I call him Jah
My God talk patois

King James version suit Englishman
For I version, fit I-man
My God talk patois
That is why I call him Jah
My God talk patois

My God is a man because I am one
God as woman, valid option
God is open to interpretation
In my slightly agnostic opinion
Everyone needs a little religion
Even atheists have rites of disposition
Pray a prayer for their conversion
I am not here to preach a sermon
Just to re-iterate this one
Religious stipulation
My God talk patois
That is why I call him Jah
My God talk patois

I don't need an interpreter
To help me with my prayer
Jah know my God talk patois
My God talk patois

A god who speaks a strange language
Is bound to be a god of bondage
My God talk patois
My God talk patois
And, whether robe or frock
My God is black

JUST DON'T WANT TO BE HUNGRY

I don't care
Who eats junk food every day
Or who needs a raise of pay
Don't care if you stay or run away
Only one ting I have to say
I just don't want to be hungry
No, I don't intend to starve

No fancy wish, no big English
Not too stylish, no gourmet dish
Even little bread and fish
Food on my plate, plain and straight
Jesus Christ, even he had to eat
Don't you see-It?
Hunger should be against the law
Ask Jack Sprat and his wife
Food is the staff of life
Yes, in God we trust
But, food is a must
And I just, don't want to be hungry
No, I don't intend to starve

I don't care
What type of clothes people wear
Don't care who does what with their hair
Or drinks too much beer
Don't care, I don't care, I don't care

Don't care which music gets the most airplay
And who is straight or who is gay
I don't care about election day
Don't care how people pray
Or what god they obey
That's okay
Only one ting I have to say
I just don't want to be hungry
And I won't roll over and starve

POEMSTORM

No time to be calm like Uncle Tom
Silence can harm
Ring alarm, turn on charm
World history to perform
In a poemstorm

Silence is a crime at this time
Awake and arise
Come make a worldwide noise!
Words on their own
Can crush flesh and bone
Like stick and stone

Have poems, don't need any gun
Open fire with teeth and tongue
I won't be calm like Uncle Tom
My mouth is my firearm
Word history to perform
In a poemstorm, in a poemstorm
In a poemstorm

Vocal stylings like hurricane winds
Force of voices can change things
Wordsounds have power
Voices must utter, silence to shatter
From gutter to control tower
Exercise choice, blaze voice
Vaporize the ice

Don't be calm like Uncle Tom
But use your mouth, not a firearm

Many nations to transform
In a poemstorm, in a poemstorm
In a rubadub poemstorm

MI CYAAN BELIEVE IT YET

I want to bawl blood
Want to chant badwud
Nyam iron, chaw fire
Drink my own eyewater
Murder, murder
Murder uppa Stony Hill
Mikey Smith get kill

I can't forget, can't stop grieve yet
Mikey Smith, dubpoet, stoned to death
Lawd ... mi cyaan believe it yet!

Yuh noh see-it Trainer
Mikey was a dream planter
Streetpsalms chanter
Wordwarrior, soulhealer
Truths and rights utterer
Born down a Jones Town
Us'd to flash some strong soun

I can't forget, can't stop grieve yet
Mikey Smith, dubpoet, stoned to death
Lawd ... mi cyaan believe it yet!

Spokenword revolution
Mikey put it in motion
Worldwide attention, honorebel mention
Paris, Munich, New York, London
Dubbing with Linton, "Upon Westminster Bridge"
Us'd to par with C.L.R.
Trading knowledge, university college

Mikey was mighty, but not highty-tighty
Used to be sprightly, used to shine brightly
Big buff-teeth smile, cool profile
Dropshort walk, fullheart talk
Mikey Smith was poor people poet
Yet is not rich people stone him to death
Lawd ... mi cyaan believe it yet!

JOHNNY REBEL

Hey, Tommy Trouble!
Did you know Johnny Rebel?
Disciple of the Devil
Mr. Miserable, dreadful and terrible
The intolerable Johnny Rebel
Was a crack baby
Mommy O.D. after delivery
Daddy dead at age twenty
Poor sick old granny was his security
She died before he reach'd puberty
With only a gang for family
Johnny became his own worst enemy

The gun was his skill
It gave him a thrill to rob and kill
Deadly, dangerous and notorious
The intolerable Johnny Rebel
Vessel of hate and rage
Soon hit front page
Daily News! Daily News
Robert Rankin, alias Johnny Rebel
Wanted, dead ... and not alive ...
He really couldn't survive

Hunt'd like a beast
Johnny knew no peace
Taste of a threat in every breath
Immediate prospect of death
No sleep on the run
His only friend was his gun

Killer cops on the case
Hot on the chase, marked his face
Set up a trap at Miss Fanny foodshop
Say, who is that?
Ratta-tat-tat
Guess what?
Before he could fire shot Johnny get drop

Fresh dead-meat on sidewalk concrete
Blood-tinted teeth, cycle complete
Public sigh of relief, not one cry of grief
Only the sky weeps a little, for Johnny Rebel

COLD BLUES ON THE ROCKS

Even tireless dreams
Sometimes trip over their own tracks
Life is a diet of harsh facts
Time, always busy collecting tax
And it's not easy to relax
Sipping cold blues on the rocks

MARLEY VIBES

Bend Down Low
Mek me tell you what I know
Singer gone, songs live on
Ites Rasta, *Buffalo Soldier*
Duppy Conqueror, conqueror!
I still see his face all over the place

Crazy Baldheads lost in haste
Souls going to waste
Fleeting illusions they chase

Forget the Rat Race
Natty Dread drum and bass
Change pace in *a rubadub style*
I still hear Bob Marley wailing
Don't you hear him?
Stilla sing, ah sing, deh sing
Strong songs of sufferers *Uprising*
Chanting
Rastaman Vibrations for all nations
Roots rock reggae
Rebel Music of a Natural Mystic
Keeps us *Easy Scanking* thru concrete jungles
Voicing versions of *Redemption Song*

My mind is my kingdom
I am talking freedom
Feel it in the One-Drop
Blues, jazz, soul, funk
Disco, hiphop
Dance across generation gap
Rainfall wet every house-top
Rasta don't rap no crap

Yes, I remember
When we used to walk and look
A little food to cook
Paying our dues, *Talking Blues*

In a tenement yard down a *shantytown*
Mi seh we *draw Bad Card*
Sometimes sleeping on *cold ground*
There we taste dubsound
So Much Things To Say
Too much gunplay
When all is said and done
I'm gonna stare in the sun
My voice is my gun
That is more than just a pun
If a fire mek it bun
If a blood mek it run

I and *I don't want to Wait In Vain*
To take *Zion Train*
Natty Dread, Rides Again
Riding with Jah guide
Rasta ride rite thru
Ambush, Roadblock, Curfew

Movements of Jah people
Stepping into *Exodus*
Leaving *Babylon, By Bus*
I heard *the street people talking*
Heard them saying
After you've done your praying
Get Up, Stand Up for your right
Africans Unite
Shake off *hypocrite and parasite*
Let's lift our heads and give Jah praises!
Wake Up And Live

Here I come again
Making music out of pain
Another *black survivor*
Coming In From The Cold
We are the children of those who were sold
So long we've been pushing plow
Time for harvest now

Two thousand years of history
Could not be wiped away so easily
Give us the teachings of His Majesty
We don't want *the Devil's philosophy*
No more *mental slavery*
Tell the children the truth
Babylon Sistim is a vampire
Sucking the blood of the sufferer
Innocent blood, shed every day
Someone will have to pay
I say, *Revolution* without salvation
Is no solution
Johnny Was a good man

So much sorrow in the world
Too much trouble in the world!
Many more will have to suffer
Many more will have to die
Don't ask I and I why
Gunshots don't tell lie
But, *No Woman, No Cry*
Don't even sigh
Just hold your head high
And praise Jah Rastafari

Forget your sadness and dance
Forget the distress and dance!
Cast away the fears
Don't let your dreams drown in tears
When the morning gathers the rainbow
Arise and let the world know
You are also a rainbow

The Sun Is Shining
Dark clouds have silver lining
To the rescue
Another mighty Marleysong
Don't worry, about a thing
Little darling, stop grieving
Keep on believing, we'll be *Jamming*
One Bright Morning

In sweet togetherness singing
One Love, one heart
Let's get together and feel all right

Even if, *everywhere is War*
Chances Are
Every little thing's gonna be all right
Every little thing's gonna be all right
So Jah Seh

COW AN GOAT STYLE

Ketch dis quick, wi got nuff muzik
FireHouse van, come-een nuh don
Nuh badda tek no Quawta Million
Woman stop fuss an step up inna di bus
Ah mussi badwud yuh want mi cuss
No more schoolaz, lick shat drivah

Tek off faas wid di tape full blaas
Minibus ride inna cow an goat style
Wickid an wile, keep yuh frettin evri mile

Conduckta beerly heng-on pon di door
Dem still deh stop fi tek up more
Di bus pak suh tite, passinjaz out fi fite
Hey man, watch weh yuh deh put yuh han
Eskuze mi ma'am, is mi corntoe yuh stan-up pon
Miss Matty
Beg yuh tek yuh ten ton batty offa mi baby
Granny moov di luggige
Peeple, oonu step up in di pussige
Lawd wat a heet
Sumadi gi di baby-madda a seet
Massa nuh worry feel-up mi packit
Not ev'n bus-fare nuh inna it
Lawd look weh mi neerly get jook wid ice-prik
Drivah beg yuh tern awf dat dutty muzik
My Gad ... mi stumuck sik
Agony, agony, pon di journey
Jah kno seh di swet smell strang
An someone raise a sang
Nearah my Gaawd to deeee
Drivah is kill yuh deh try kill wi
Lawd is suh im tek di corna wide
Lady, beg yuh tek yuh elbow outa mi side

Minibus ride inna cow an goat style
Wickid an wile, keep yuh frettin evri mile

Missa Duckta, why yuh pak-up di bus suh
Like seh people ah cargo
Lady if yuh nuh likey go tek taxi
Peeple, oonu come inna di van.
Oonu nuh see poleesman
Bus-stop, bus stop
But stap, BUS STAPP
Eeze di squeeze, all fares pleeze
T'ank God fi sum fresh breeze
Spin it roun, downtown

Minibus ride
Inna cow an goat style
Wickid an wile
Keep yuh frettin evri mile
An yuh nah smile
Yuh feel like yuh deh bwile
Mood spwile, clothes sile
Inna cow an goat style
Diss a
Cow an goat
Style

GLIMPSES AND GLANCES

Winter chilled winds blow
Moonglow on virgin snow
Warmth was yesterday
Gardens of the sun where I used to play

Nose stiffened, fingers on fire
Swaddled in layers of survival
Shovelling for poems on frostbitten deck
Fragments of the past I recollect
Things I cannot forget
Sunshine creased into memories
Smiling waves, sunglazed sea
Sunlight supreme, a snowbird's dream

Winds at rest, catching breath
Shivering night frozen into tight
Eloquence shimmering semi-silence
Solitude speaks and I write
Mute trees mock my musings
Imaging the frigid beauty of rigid lakes
I wish I'd learned to dance on skates

Shapes of spaces, moods of places
Glimpses and glances
Eroded distances

Merged emotions lodged between words
My heart draped in two flags
It is big enough for both places
Places, places in spaces
Spaces, spaces of places
Places and spaces

Leafless maples stand on guard

Shuddering snowman in my front yard
Snowsuited someone wagged by their dog
Tracks of snow boots in the park
So much snow seems so stark

First day of winter, I'm a snowflake catcher
Next day of winter, I'm a weather watcher
Too bad I can't buy my ticket to fly

Winter soundtrack
Summer flashback
Aunt Dass feeding the big fat sow
Uncle Alpheus chasing down a cow

Right now, over there
It's Bermuda shorts, not winter gear
I was raised where
One type of wear works all year
There winter, spring, summer and fall
Look too close to call

RANT AGAINST OTHERNESS

Creation, evolution
Single foundation
Earth is our mother
There is no other
Just sister and brother
People shouldn't have to bother
About being the other
Other
(Othering no!
Togetherness yes!
The poor could make more
If the rich would take less

Between right and wrong
Where does love belong?
Equality, compssion
Buzzwords in a slogan
Majority, minority
Unbalanced democracy
Tellurian alien, otherization
Position, opposition
Policies of exclusion
Domination by division
Othering by stigma
Problematic agenda
Social wilderness of otherness
Others othering to oppress
Outcries of togetherness?

(   )

Animal is natural, normal is cultural
And I do believe that God is neutral
There is a link between red and pink
After all the queering, find time for sharing
Actual people viewed together
Universal, but particular
Different, yet similar

Intersections always exist
Injustice we must resist

Erase racism, sexism and classism
Delete adultism, ageism and ableism
Disable all isms
Decontaminate capitalism
Ostracize othering
Othering, othering
Othering no!
Togetherness yes!
The poor could make more
If the rich would take less

LITERARY COUP

In my view, a military coup
Could only empower a few
It's better to do a literary coup
Literary coup, this literary coup
Is too huge to be a haiku

Entry point of no return
Mutiny of the subaltern
Postmodern pith and pattern
Profile of a superaltern
To Whom it May Concern
I think it's my turn
To teach and you learn

Mosquito one, mosquito two
Mosquito jump in the hot callaloo
Cocka-doodle doo! Déjà vu
This is not voodoo, it's a literary coup

High brow, low brow
No, I don't think so
Narratives of alternatives
Overthrow, underthrow
Throw out, topple, trample
Restructure pyramid and triangle
Turn everything into a circle
Reshuffle the puzzle into a miracle
It's time to do a literary coup

World widening web, web widened world
Pages of ages further unfurled
Behold the emperor striking a pose
Doesn't seem as if he knows
We can see through his clothes

Who is who? I will dub you a clue
Penguins can't fly where the cuckoo flew
Phantoms skew the critic's review

Cocka-doodle doo! Déjà vu
This is not voodoo, it's a literary coup
As fresh as new, vintage brew
Literary coup, this literary coup
Didn't come out of the blue
It is long overdue

OPERATION TRANSLOCATION

SUMADI MUS KNO MI NAME (Root Version)

Sumadi mus kno mi name
Mus kno mi name
Dem mus kno mi name
Wha mi name?
Wha mi name?
Wha mi name?
Mi name, mi name
Mi name Rastafari

Meet mi eye to eye
Tell mi why a girl or a guy
Would really try fi sell mi samfie
As if dem cyaan identify
That I an I never drop from sky
Don't have to copy anybody identiti
Everybody born as sumadi
Sumadi, sumadi
Sumadi mus kno mi name
Mus kno mi name
Dem mus kno mi name

Blackskin, whitename
Yesideh slayve game
Slayve game, slayve game
Slavye game ah nuh fi mi shame
Tumarrow cyaan get blame
Tiddeh mi deh mek mi claim
Sumadi mus kno mi name
Mus kno mi name
Dem mus kno mi name

Four hundred years of slayvri
Wuz only
A shawt likkle pawt a fi mi stori
Fi mi identiti nevva wash weh inna sea
My hi-storee 'tretch from Sandy Gully
To Greater Zimbabwe
Sumadi mus kno me!

SOMEBODY MUST KNOW MY NAME (Translated Version)

Somebody must know my name
Must know my name
They must know my name
What's my name?
What's my name?
What's my name?
My name, my name
My name is Rastafari

Meet me eye to eye
Tell me why a girl or a guy
Would really try to sell me a lie
As if they can't identify
That my people and I didn't drop from the sky
Don't have to copy anybody's identity
Everybody was born as somebody
Somebody, somebody
Somebody must know my name
Must know my name
They must know my name

Black skin, white name
Yesterday's slave game
Slave game, slave game
Slave game is not my shame
Tomorrow can't be blamed
Today I am making my claim
Somebody must know my name
Must know my name
They must know my name

Four hundred years of slavery
Was only
A short little part of my story
My identity wasn't washed away by the sea
My high-story stretches from Sandy Gully
To Greater Zimbabwe
Somebody must know me!

SUMADI MUS KNO MI NAME (Dubbled Version)
SOMEBODY MUST KNOW MY NAME

Sumadi mus kno mi name
Somebody must know my name
Mus kno mi name
Must know my name
Dem mus kno mi name
They must know my name
Wha mi name?
What's my name?
Wha mi name?
What's my name?
Wha mi name?
What's my name?
Mi name, mi name
My name, my name
Mi name Rastafari
My name is Rastafari

Meet mi eye to eye
Meet me eye to eye
Tell mi why a girl or a guy
Tell me why a girl or a guy
Would really try fi sell mi samfie
Would really try to sell me a lie
As if dem cyaan identify
As if they can't identify
That I an I never drop from sky
That my people and I didn't drop from the sky
Don't have to copy anybody identiti
Don't have to copy anybody's identity
Everybody born as sumadi
Everybody was born as somebody
Sumadi, sumadi
Somebody, somebody
Sumadi mus kno mi name
Somebody must know my name
Mus kno mi name
Must know my name
Dem mus kno mi name

They must know my name

Blackskin, whitename
Black skin, white name
Yesideh slayve game
Yesterday's slave game
Slayve game, slyave game
Slave game, slave game
Slayve game ah nuh fi mi shame
Slave game is not my shame
Tumarrow cyaan get blame
Tomorrow can't be blamed
Tiddeh mi deh mek mi clam
Today I am making my claim
Sumadi mus kno mi name
Somebody must know my name
Mus kno mi name
Must know my name
Dem mus kno mi name
They must know my name

Four hundred years of slayvri
Four hundred years of slavery
Wuz only
Was only
A shawt likkle pawt a fi mi stori
A short little part of my story
Fi mi identiti nevva wash weh inna sea
My identity wasn't washed away by the sea
My hi-storee 'tretch from Sandy Gully
My high-story stretches from Sandy Gully
To Greater Zimbabwe
To Greater Zimbabwe
Sumadi mus kno me!
Somebody must know me!

SOMEBODY MUST KNOW MY NAME
(Translocated Version)

Somebody must know my name
Must know my name
They must know my name
What's my name?
What's my name?
What's my name?

Meet me eye to eye
Tell me why any girl or guy
Would even try to bother with the lie
That I am a born stranger
With whom they can't identify
As if they don't know that I know
That I am somebody
Somebody
Somebody must know my name

Must know my name
They must know my name
My name, my name
My name is not really my name
Black skin, white name
Came from yesterday's slave game

Yesterday's slave game
Yesterday's slave game
Yesterday's slave game was not my shame
Tomorrow is free from blame
Today is my time to stake a claim
Somebody must know my name!

Four hundred years of slavery
Was only a short little part of my story
My identity wasn't lost at sea
My hi-stories stretch
From Sandy Gully to Greater Zimbabwe
I refuse to be a nonentity

nder to obscurity
now me!

REVERIE

ODE TO THE BAMBOO

i often wish i were like you
Bamboo, bamboo
Trees clustered at ease
Swishing and swaying
Choreographies of breeze
No parents to please
And no shoes to squeeze
You, Bamboo, bamboo
Lips of leaves humming
Serenity is the song you sing
In tune with everything
Bamboo, bamboo
No stiffness in your stance
Your life is a dance Bamboo
Bamboo melodies sprinkled on the wind
No moaning, no groaning
No fears of the axe in the morning
No tears for the flames in the evening
Bamboo, bamboo
Oh, look at you!
Just another clump of bamboo
Without surnames
No birthday parties for you
No loving to do, no point of view
Bamboo, bamboo
Midnight or noon, you sing the same tune
And maybe soon
Some men will come to cut you down
For things to make for sale downtown
But you never look blue
And nothing ever seems to bother you
Bamboo, Bamboo
Who can tell
What you would tell
If you could tcll
The things i think i hear
From you, a mere
Clump of
Bamboo Bamboo

THE CAGED BIRD STILL SINGS
For Maya Angelou

No sight of sky
No height
Nor width to fly
Yet the caged bird still sings
Still sings, still sings
The caged bird still sings
Soaring above misgivings
Singing
Dreamsongs to which it clings
The caged bird still sings
Glad tidings of freebird things
It sings, it sings, it sings!
Mighty hymns of wind-riding wings
The caged bird still sings
Still sings, still sings
Singing as if ...
The ceiling is the sky
Singing as if ...
To sing is to fly
The caged bird still sings
Still sings, still sings
The caged bird still sings

ACKNOWLEDGEMENTS

In general, I thank God, parents, family, publisher, editor, supporters, relatives and friends in priority sequence. Specifically, I must name three people who I wish had lived to see this book: Aunt Dass, Aunt Ell, and Janet Johnson. Additionally, I have to name five other people who have supported me closely, not only as the poet dubbing onstage but also offstage where I am merely just another vulnerable person. May God continue to bless you my beloved mother, Sylvia Braham, my mother-in-law, Sybil Longman, and three of my strongest supporters: Duncan Cruickshank, Mary Blume and Ian Gibbons.

Jah bless the people, in all the countless places in Jamaica, whose unbridled enthusiasm for dubpoetry really nurtured me. Most of all, I give thanks to Cornwall College and Mico Teachers' College where I learned to enjoy literary splendour. Blessings for the people in Swansea, Wales, who welcomed me with open ears and agreed that I have "world history to perform in a poemstorm." Hackney and Brixton, England, thanks for supporting me too. Also, of course, God bless the wonderful people of America in places like Brooklyn, Manhattan, Harlem, New Jersey, Philadelphia, Atlanta, Cleveland, and most of all, the University of Miami, where I spent two of the best summers of my life.

Here in Canada, I say hail to people in Hamilton, Dundas, Burlington, Oakville, Port Credit, Brampton, Brantford, Cambridge, Guelph, Kitchener, Waterloo, Windsor and Toronto: especially in the St. Clair West community. Outside of Ontario, I give thanks to KalmUnity and Montreal. Thanks too to those with whom I've poemized in a bus, on a train or plane … on the beach, down the lane, on a sidewalk, in the park, onstage, backstage, offstage, on a factory floor, or in a grocery store. Furthermore, if we met in a classroom, if I taught you, or were taught by you, I have learned from you. If I listened to you, or talked to you, I gained something from you. Perhaps, I borrowed an echo, a glimpse, glance, gesture, wink, sigh, smile, chuckle, or turn of phrase from you; I give thanks. Then, there is another special line of gratitude for my editor, Lillian Allen, and her generosity in lending me her idea of doubling a poem. The result is presented in the Operation Translocation section of the book.

The members and staff of the Dub Poets Collective deserve an extra special salute. Each one helped to improve this book in some way or another. Sandra Alland, McGilligan's copy-editor, deserves honourable mention for her thoroughness. I tried my best to frame my dubpoetic license within the parameters of her sense of consistency, except in cases like "getto" and "ghetto," where variance denotes shifts in perspective.

At this point, it is my pleasure to voice a special shoutout to the white dubpoetry enthusiasts who were the first Hamiltonians to embrace and support me with PoeMagic, extra gratitude to those who volunteered their time and energy to consistently promote the event. Thanks to owners and regulars of Gallery 435, Staircase and Blue Angel Gallery, for willingly providing venues. Much respect is due also, to the black supporters who quickly caught on and made each Black History Month edition of PoeMagic always enormously well-attended and extremely memorable in Hamilton, Ontario, Canada, where I live, a long way from Delveland, Jamaica, the place of my birth, where this book really began.

So now, after I hail the Jamaica Foundation of Hamilton; I must honour the 'Delvelanders,' who participated in those glorious Eighties community-based performances. Sistren and bredrin of the dream, I am making some noise for you. Finally, to the reader, I give thanks for your attention.

KLYDE BROOX — a.k.a. Durm-I — is an internationally sea-
soned dub poet with decades of performance experience in
North America, Europe and the Caribbean. Born in Jamaica,
Klyde left high school to teach and perform as a poet. He
won the Nathan Brissett Poetry Competition in 1978, and
was soon a recognized regular on the burgeoning Jamaican
poetry performance scene. One of Jamaica's most promis-
ing dub poets, he traveled to England and the United States
for readings, workshops, and guest lectures. His chapbook,
"Poemstorm," was released in 1989. In 1992, Klyde received
a James Michener Fellowship to the University of Miami Car-
ibbean Writers Summer Institute. A scholarship followed in
1993, and Klyde migrated to Canada that same year, set-
tling in Hamilton, Ontario. In 2004, he was nominated for a
John C. Holland Award for community service. Klyde works
in arts development with the Toronto-based Dub Poets Col-
lective, and hosts Poemagic, a popular performance-oriented
open-mic series in Hamilton, where he lives with his family.